pray like this

CHRIST'S GUIDE TO PRAYING THE SCRIPTURES

KATIE NOBLE

FREE GIFT
sample chapter

A Note From

THE EDITOR

We launched Hosanna Revival Publishing in 2020 with this very book, *Pray Like This: Christ's Guide to Praying the Scriptures*, written by Katie Noble. In one sense, we had no idea what we were getting ourselves into. We had little experience in the world of publishing, and we were very much figuring things out as we went. In another sense, we had a crystal clear vision of what Hosanna Revival Publishing would look like. *Pray Like This* is a wonderful example of that vision, and in a way, is our "flagship" devotional. It is a beautiful book written for our community by our community, and it immerses readers in the Scriptures, pointing them to Jesus.

This sample copy is our free gift to you, and it contains the introduction and first week of devotional content in this study of the Lord's Prayer from Matthew 6. The Lord's Prayer is our prayer—God is our Father. We pray you will enjoy this free gift and consider purchasing the full book.

Will Burrows
Director of Publishing, Hosanna Revival

For Dave, my harbor and Hank and Johnny, my sails.

Table of
CONTENTS

Table of

CONTENTS

A Note From

THE AUTHOR

Dear Reader,

You're familiar, I'm sure, with breaking points—those moments when you've nothing to do but throw up your hands and surrender to what's in front of you, for better or worse. In the journey to spiritual adulthood, it is God's mercy to bring us to our breaking point sooner than later.

Mine came shortly after the birth of my oldest son. I had been a Christian for more than a decade, having met Jesus quite early in life. I'd gone by the book: went to Sunday school and summer camps, prayed "the prayer" at least twice, volunteered countless hours to bring the gospel of Jesus to students in my community, married a missionary, and faithfully served the local church. Then I had a baby and found myself running on fumes. My well of spiritual energy was bone dry. I was crippled by insecurity, desperately seeking belonging and groundedness in the affirmation of others, personal achievements, and external image. I longed for a leisurely spirit, the abounding peace of God—but I didn't have it. Doing all the "right things" had not afforded me the deep intimacy with God I needed in order to calm down and grow up.

Then our pastor and dear friend mentioned to us that we'd be walking through the Lord's Prayer as a church. *The Lord's*

Prayer? I thought with arrogance. *I suppose that will be helpful for new believers.* Like many of you, I had memorized the Lord's Prayer as a child and thought it no more than a sing-song poem for Christian beginners. But as we began to wade through the deep riches of this incredible gift, I came undone. My soul began to sing. This simple prayer was the key I had been searching for, and I had been holding it all along. No amount of authenticity or willpower could have taught me what Christ's prayer has. I have spent nearly two years studying this ancient path, and I've only begun to plumb the depths of it. I am honored that you'd join me on this journey toward Jesus, our redeemer and friend. If you find yourself at a breaking point, these words are precisely for you. May he bless and keep you as we grow up together, in him and with him.

I owe one million thanks to my friends at Hosanna Revival for making space for me to do this work; to the women of The Bearcave for holding my hand as I stumbled my way through; to my family, for everything; to The Oaks Community Church, for loving and raising me; and to my precious Savior for the unspeakable gift of prayer and your patience with me as I figure it out. You are so kind to us.

katie noble

pray then like this
Our Father in heaven
hallowed be your name
Your Kingdom come,
your will be done
On Earth as it is in heaven.
Give us this day our daily bread.
And forgive us our debts,
as we also have forgiven our debtors.
And lead us not into temptation,
but deliver us from the evil one.

INTRODUCTION

Prayer is the soul's sincere desire,
uttered or unexpressed;
the motion of a hidden fire
that trembles in the breast.

Prayer is the burden of a sigh,
the falling of a tear;
the upward glancing of an eye
when none but God is near.

Prayer is the simplest form of speech
that infant lips can try,
prayer the sublimest strains that reach
the Majesty on high.

Prayer is the Christian's vital breath,
the Christian's native air,
his watchword at the gates of death:
he enters heaven with prayer.

Prayer is the contrite sinner's voice,
returning from his ways;
while angels in their songs rejoice,
and cry, 'Behold, he prays!

The saints in prayer appear as one,
in word and deed and mind;
while with the Father and the Son
sweet fellowship they find.

Nor prayer is made on earth alone:
the Holy Spirit pleads,
and Jesus on the eternal throne
for sinners intercedes.

O Thou by whom we come to God,
the Life, the Truth, the Way,
the path of prayer thyself hast trod:
Lord, teach us how to pray!

Prayer Is The Soul's Sincere Desire

James Montgomery, 1818

INTRODUCTION

Pray Like This

We are, by nature, praying creatures—restless children who find peace finally and fully in the steadfast love of our heavenly Father. For years, I misunderstood prayer to be a Christian's endeavor to draw near to God, as an appointment to let him know what it is I need. In reality, the inverse is true: prayer is our invitation to realize that all this time God has been drawing near to us, speaking to us, meeting our needs before we knew to ask. As Henri Nouwan put it, prayer is

"The place in which you can listen to the voice of the One who calls you the beloved. To pray is to listen to the One who calls you 'my beloved daughter,' 'my beloved son,' 'my beloved child.' To pray is to let that voice speak to the center of your being, to your guts, and let that voice resound in your whole being."

It is true that prayer can be a kind of conversation with God, but until we realize that God initiates the conversation, we're likely approaching the discipline incorrectly. More than conversation, though, prayer is a means of communion—more of a place than a presentation. The place of prayer is where we bring our dreams, longings, fears, and sorrows to be realigned, reformed, healed, and restored. It is where our souls find what they've been searching for all along: home.

So how do we pray? What do we say? What are we to ask for? How are we to posture ourselves? Well, Jesus gives us the answer in Matthew 6:9-13:

"Pray then like this:
'Our Father in heaven,
hallowed be your name.
Your kingdom come,
your will be done,
on earth as it is in heaven.
Give us this day our daily bread,
and forgive us our debts,
as we also have forgiven our debtors.
And lead us not into temptation,
but deliver us from the evil one.'"[1]

Of course, there is infinite room for us to explore God's presence in prayer and no singular "correct" way to pray. But Jesus, in his mercy, did give us a template. And we are wise to follow his lead.

The Lord's Prayer is not a rubric for beginners, nor a checkbox for the rule followers. It is a practice in praying the scriptures. As it's translated to English, the Lord's Prayer is made up of 57 words, ten phrases, each of which direct us deep into doctrine scattered throughout the Bible. It makes sense that Jesus, the incarnate Word, would give us a prayer rooted in God's eternal truth. Dr. Timothy Keller remarks that in praying the Lord's Prayer, we are effectively praying all of Scripture.[2] As we anchor our prayers in the Word of God, we relinquish the childish belief that prayer is best dictated by our fleeting emotions and desires. Instead we begin the work of aligning our loves and longings to those of Christ and humbly admit that ours are in desperate need of reformation. To pray the Scriptures is to plant our feet on the firm foundation of God-reality. And all this abundance is kindly offered to us in so modest a package.

Why The

LORD'S PRAYER

WHY

The Lord's Prayer

The understatement of the Lord's Prayer—its sheer lack of length and frill—may be a holdup to some. We may believe God pays closer attention to long, elaborate prayers swollen with "Christian" vocabulary. But as Jesus teaches just prior to the Lord's Prayer, the true marks of Christian prayer are privacy and simplicity:

"And when you come before God, don't turn that into a theatrical production either. All these people making a regular show out of their prayers, hoping for fifteen minutes of fame! Do you think God sits in a box seat?

"Here's what I want you to do: Find a quiet, secluded place so you won't be tempted to role-play before God. Just be there as simply and honestly as you can manage. The focus will shift from you to God, and you will begin to sense his grace" (Matthew 6:5-6 MSG).

Others of us may believe a prayer we memorized in Sunday school to be too elementary to bear the weight of our complex adult lives. But, in God's wisdom and compassion, Jesus upholds a childlike faith—one that humbly accepts prayers easy to remember when the temptations and storms of life threaten to swallow us whole.

"Mark this: Unless you accept God's kingdom in the simplicity of a child, you'll never get in" (Mark 10:15 MSG).

Still others of us get itchy at the idea of accepting someone else's template for something as personal and intimate as prayer. Imitation (which, by the way, is a pillar of discipleship)[3] is regarded as cheap fraudulence in our age of authenticity. But let's consider whose lead we're following: Jesus Christ, our loving Savior, who paved a way to God through his very own body; Jesus Christ, the incarnate Word of God, whose character revealed the exact imprint of the Father's glory. We do well to relent in our crusade for authenticity when the one we're imitating is Christ. His way is better, higher, and truer than ours, and it meets needs we don't yet know we have.

The Lord's Prayer is Jesus' invitation to learn who God is, what he loves, and how we are to relate to him as his children. And while we're at it, let's lay down our expectations, too. Prayer is not an occasion to impress God, nor is it an opportunity to impress others. It is not a discipline with grade levels or graduation. It is not a space to prove our individuality. It is a sacred space of communion with our heavenly Father who knows what we need and who we are. He is the one who made us. We are free to come before him with honesty and simplicity.

How to Use This

DEVOTIONAL

HOW TO USE THIS DEVOTIONAL

And other suggested practices

In the coming weeks, we will excavate the Lord's Prayer phrase by phrase. Each of the ten phrases is rooted in huge swathes of Biblical principle, which we'll examine one by one.* Many of the questions included for consideration do not have a "correct" answer; so don't fret over accuracy. The goal is deeper awareness of God, self, and the Scriptures.

Our study of each phrase will end with a "Pray Like This" application worksheet. On these pages, you'll find a version of the familiar ACTS prayer. This rhythm aims to tie all we've learned about God, the world, and ourselves in the previous few days together.

ACTS is an acronym for the essential elements of prayer as outlined in the Lord's Prayer: Adoration, Confession, Thanksgiving, Supplication. I've modified it a bit to include repentance, lament, and commitment. The acronym remains the same.

ADORATION: *The act of exalting God, proclaiming his character, glory and faithfulness. It is essential that we begin and end our prayer focused expressly on God himself.*

CONFESSION, REPENTANCE, AND LAMENT: *It's natural to become aware of our wickedness as we remember God's holiness and beauty. Here, we confess sin honestly and specifically. To repent is to actively turn from sin; to intentionally choose the path of righteousness. Lament is the act of bringing sorrow before God, pouring out our brokenness, heartache, fear, and grief in faith that he hears and sees.*

THANKSGIVING: *Gratitude is the posture in which we offer all of our prayers.*[4] *Thank him for what he's done, what he's doing, and what he's promised to accomplish. In humility, we seek to receive his truth, love, and peace day by day and praise him for the blessings and healing he bought with his blood.*

SUPPLICATION: *We are free to ask God to continue to bless and heal us. Bring these unmet needs and desires before God. Pray for others, too.*

COMMITMENT: *Decide how your prayer will be worked out in your life today: how might your prayer be "metabolized" into the works of your hands and feet? Ask the Spirit to embolden and equip you for this work.*

I also suggest you commit to praying the Lord's Prayer word for word every day at a regularly scheduled time. I practice this each morning while I wait for my coffee to brew. You may practice it before a meal, as you get ready for work, alone or with a spouse. Forming any new habit requires time and discipline. We cannot expect to run a marathon without training our body any more than we can expect ourselves to develop a rich, mature prayer life without making a plan and sticking to it. As you form this new rhythm of worship, remember that it does not make you more holy or more worthy of the un-earnable grace of Christ. Praying this prayer each day will not make God love you more; it will not earn you extra spiritual brownie points. What it will do is anchor you to a rhythm of prayer that will frame your days, seasons, and entire life in awareness of and service to the gospel.

 I encourage you to work through this series of devotions at your own pace and to take days off if you need them. This is not a race; it is a Spirit-led journey of spiritual discipline and prayer.

*Please note that this type of scattered Scripture reading is not a proper substitute for regular, contextual study of the Bible. While I've done much work to ensure we are not pulling the Scriptures away from their original intention to prove my point, it is ultimately up to you—the disciple—to search the Scriptures' true meaning. If reading the Bible is a new practice for you, or you're stuck on how to continue to grow in this practice, I recommend Jen Wilkin's book, *Women of the Word: How to Study the Bible with Both Our Hearts and Our Minds*, and her library of stunning Bible studies. You can find them on her website, jenwilkin.net.

DROP A PIN: Examine your current prayer life.

Before we begin, let's examine our current prayer lives. If taking a high-level view of your entire life of prayer is too much, condense your investigation to the past seven days.

How do you most commonly address God? What name(s) do you give him in prayer?

Acknowledge any holdups you have surrounding the Lord's Prayer. Does it seem too simple, too elementary, inauthentic?

What are you currently asking from God?

For yourself

For loved ones

For the world

When do you pray? How frequently and in what circumstance(s)?

What do you find yourself confessing, repenting of, and/or lamenting?

How do your relationships play into your life of prayer?

What current obstacles can you identify to your growth in the discipline of prayer?

Can you recall prayers you've seen answered recently?

What areas of growth in your prayer life can you identify? How do you wish to see your prayer life changed?

Then all my servant works were done
A righteousness to raise;
Now, freely chosen in the Son,
I freely choose his ways.

To see the law by Christ fulfilled
And hear his pardoning voice,
Changes a slave into a child,
And duty into choice.

Love Constraining to Obedience
William Cowper

PART ONE

Our Father

IN HEAVEN

Introduction

Our God—the Creator of the cosmos, Giver and Sustainer of life, Alpha and Omega—could have chosen anything in the universe as his preferred title. His choice: our Father. Not only the Father of Christ the Righteous, but the Father of each adopted son and daughter who would call upon his holy name. How might deep intimacy with "the theme of heaven's praises"[5]—our heavenly Father—change the way we pray? How might it change the way we live, and the way we relate to one another?

DAY ONE:

OUR FATHER

Daddy Issues

Read: Galatians 3:23-29

Before we jump into the fatherhood of God, let's consider to whom his fatherhood belongs. When Jesus spoke this prayer, he was the only begotten Son of God; the only living thing righteous enough to claim God as his Father. So, it would have made sense for Jesus to open this prayer with "My Father." Instead, he prays, "Our Father;" "our" meaning his and yours and mine. Jesus looks forward to the unconditional love, full access, new identity, and absolute protection he'd buy for us, his adopted brothers and sisters, on the cross. By praying "Our Father," Jesus invites us to pray as members of God's united forever family.

Radical oneness of believers, though beautiful in theory, can be rocky in practice. We have difficulty celebrating God's love, access, identity, and protection as it's offered to members of a denomination whose worship makes us uncomfortable; to believers whose faith seems too small or too radical; to those Christians who think and vote and speak very differently from us; to men and women who have sinned so heinously that Jesus the righteous had to bleed and die to make atonement (that's all of us). Beginning our prayers by addressing our Father reminds us just how far his grace can reach.

Jesus' opening words also remind us that though we pray in secret, we never truly pray alone.[6] Each prayer we offer to God joins others uttered by all the adopted sons and daughters who would publicly claim his righteousness through baptism and a life of faith. Our voice joins the chorus of the beloved, calling out to their Father in heaven.

In prayer, consider the following questions:

Who do you have trouble imagining in the family of God? Which members of your spiritual family do you tend to discount because they seem too much or not enough? Whose worship makes you uncomfortable and why?

How might acknowledging and pursuing unity with your spiritual brothers and sisters change the way you pray? How might it change the way you think and act toward believers who worship differently than you?

DAY TWO:

OUR FATHER

Our Abba Father

Read: Romans 8:14-17

It is a common misconception that the word Abba is properly translated as "daddy," our language's most intimate phrase for father. And while Abba does imply intimacy, it is not an intimacy that dissolves as the child matures. A more accurate translation of Abba implies an intimacy borne of a gut-level, time-tested, grownup confidence in the character, promise, and love of the father. Let's allow today's text to guide us into a meditation upon God's own character, promise, and love.

Romans 8:14 says that all who are led by the _____ are children of God.

Now read John 14:15-21. What promises does Jesus make to those of us who have inherited the Spirit? What do those promises reveal about God's character? Consider your heavenly Father's care in times of trial.

With the Spirit, recall a period of suffering in which you felt the kinship of Jesus, or a time you cried out to God because you knew he was the only one who could help. What did that experience teach you?

From what do you still need delivered? Examine where else you run for help in times of need, stress, or fear. Where do you run for comfort when that temptation or pain rises up? What do those tendencies reveal about where your hope lies?

How deep the Father's love for us
How vast beyond all measure
That he should give his only Son
To make a wretch his treasure

How great the pain of searing loss
The Father turns his face away
As wounds which mar the Chosen One
Bring many sons to glory

How Deep The Father's Love For Us
Stuart Townsends

DAY FOUR:

OUR FATHER

In Heaven

Read: Romans 5:6-11, Hebrews 4:12-16

At its most basic, heaven is the current dwelling place of God: a true and present dimension full of his glory, power, and praise. Suffering, death, sickness, betrayal, deceit, jealousy, and vanity are not in heaven; they never have been and they never will be—imperfection cannot exist in the presence of God.

Heaven is where our holy Father belongs, and since we (his children) find our homes in his presence, our souls long to be there too. But sin—our attempt to find peace, joy, goodness, beauty anywhere but in God—makes us enemies of heaven. In our sin, there is no way for us to enter into the presence of God.

Sit with this reality for a few moments.

Now write Romans 5:8-10 word for word:

It is here that we realize the scandal of our adoption. God did not choose us as his sons and daughters because we bore his resemblance on our own, nor because we earned the title. He adopted us at a very great cost because it was his will. Our heavenly citizenship is proof of God's cosmic love.[7] Jesus gave up his rightful citizenship in heaven to take on our earthly citizenship, then gave that up to take up the merited citizenship of sinners: hell. And he didn't stop there! He passed through hell, defeating sin and death, in order that we might enter the gates of heaven on the basis of his righteousness. "The Son of God became man to enable men to become sons of God."[8]

Spend some time and energy thinking about your adoption into the nation of heaven. Think of what it cost Jesus to offer you this heritage. Re-read today's passages and follow the prayer outline:

Our Father in heaven, how great is your love for me! While I was still weak, still sinning, struggling with _____, you sent your Son to die for me.

But you did not stop there. you reconciled me to yourself, saved me, and set me on a new path of righteousness! I praise you for these ways my life has been radically changed in being reconciled to you: _____.

Jesus, you made a way to God where there was no way. you became like me that I may, by your grace, become like you. I can now draw near to God and his throne of mercy and ask for help. Please, Lord, help me as I _____.

Joyful, joyful, we adore Thee,

God of glory, Lord of love;

Hearts unfold like flowers before

Thee, Opening to the sun above.

Melt the clouds of sin and sadness;

Drive the dark of doubt away;

Giver of immortal gladness,

Fill us with the light of day!

Joyful, Joyful, We Adore Thee
Henry Jackson Van Dyke

PART ONE

WRAP UP

For a reminder of what each section of the ACTS
prayer means, refer back to pages 24 and 25.

A — adoration:

C — confession, repentance, lament:

T — thanksgiving:

S — supplication:

Commit:

NOTES

Pray Like This

ENDNOTES

ENDNOTES

1   Or *from evil*.

2   Timothy Keller, "Family: Our Father," September 28, 2014, *Gospel In Life Podcast*, produced by Redeemer Presbyterian Church, podcast, MP3 audio, https://gospelinlife.com/downloads/family-our-father-8596.

3   1 Corinthians 11:1

4   "Do not be anxious about anything, but in everything by prayer and supplication with thanksgiving let your requests be made known to God" (Philippians 4:6).

5   Matt Boswell, Michael Bleeker, Matt Papa, "Come Behold The Wondrous Mystery," *Look and Live*, 2012 Bleecker Publishing, Getty Music Hymns and Songs, Getty Music Publishing, Love Your Enemies Publishing, McKinney Music, Inc., 2013, track 7.

6   Stanley Hauerwas, "Matthew 6," *Matthew: Brazos Theological Commentary on the Bible*, (Ada, MI: Brazos Press, 2006), 77.

7   Philippians 3:20

8   C. S. Lewis, *Mere Christianity*, (New York: HarperCollins, 2001), 178.

About

THE BOOK

The Lord's Prayer is a rich, beautiful example of how we are to pray as Christians. Jesus began this teaching by saying, "Pray then like this...," so we would do well to heed his words. We know it's important to pray, but it can sometimes be difficult knowing *what* or *how* to pray.

Pray Like This is an 8-week study of the Lord's Prayer in Matthew 6 designed for individual or group use. Each week features Scripture reading, space for personal reflection, and an application sheet with guided prayers. Join author Katie Noble as she mines the riches of the Lord's Prayer one line at a time, drawing us nearer to the foot of the cross and teaching us a biblical language of prayer as we look to Jesus as our example. Push past any assumptions you may have about the Lord's Prayer and ask God to open your eyes to new and beautiful riches in his Word. Let it shape the way you talk to God as you learn to pray the Scriptures.

If you enjoyed this sample chapter of *Pray Like This*, the full devotional can be purchased from Hosanna Revival. To purchase your copy, visit hosannarevival.com/praylikethisbook, or scan the QR code below.

Hosanna Revival

PUBLISHING

Hosanna Revival Publishing was launched in August 2020 as a way to provide our community with rich Bible study and devotional content written by our community. Our mission has always been to excite people about engaging with Scripture by creating beautiful and intentional tools for their lives, and Hosanna Revival Publishing does exactly that. We work side by side with authors and aspiring authors from our community to create beautiful devotionals and Bible studies to help people engage more deeply with Jesus and his Word.

USE CODE:

2FOR30

To purchase two devotionals for $30

"Offer valid for a limited time only"

SCAN THE QR CODE TO SHOP ALL OF OUR DEVOTIONALS:

Other titles available from Hosanna Revival Publishing:

PRAY LIKE THIS
Katie Noble

I AM NOT IN CHARGE
Ness Cannon

SONGS FOR THE SUFFERING
Julia Allspaw

YET
Erica Boden

GOD OF FOREVER
Haylee Williams

ROOTED TO RISE
Haley Crabtree

THE STORY CIRCLE
Joshua Lenon

BEAUTY NOT BEHELD
Paige Stitt-McBride